"IQKJ"

(Inspiring Quotations Knowledgeably Justified)

Printed in the United States of America

ISBN 9781981077328

Connect with me on Twitter
@lmaoKJ
Email
Kenneth3dixon@yahoo.com

"IQKJ"

INTRODUCTION

I dedicate this third book of mines to God, my mother Michelle Jackson, family members, supportive audience and my future wife and kids. Thanks to you all for the inspiration, had it not been for y'all I probably would've stopped writing a long time ago. Thankfully, while dedicating my time to writing this book, I've heard Jim Rohn mention in a seminar of his that "Reasons can change your life, here's what else I've found out, reason come first answers come second, you don't get the answers to do well until you get the reasons. Life has a mysterious way of holding on to all the answers, and it only gives them up to the people that are inspired by reason. So reasons make the difference in how your life works out" and from that point on I knew how powerful that information was only because of how I resonated with it. I also ran across Steve Harvey words of wisdom that said "Your gift is what you do the absolute best with the least amount of effort" which helped me to appreciate this writing ability that God has gave me. Even though this inspirational writing of mines isn't in order I still have great faith and hope that it'll help those who are in need of some enlightenment in life. Thanks once again for everyone who support me, I hope you learn some valuable information about life in "IQKJ".

Write down what you've learned

1. _____

2. _____

3. _____

"IQKJ"

*"Don't let your learning lead to knowledge
you'll become a fool, let your learning lead to action
you can become wealthy" -Jim Rohn*

I nstantly after hearing this information I knew I had to do what was necessary to maintain a stable mentality and not overwhelm myself with the process of new consul. I took the thought of balancing situations in my life very seriously mainly because I never wanted to lose focus on what I had ahead of me. Ever since I read from Theodore Vail that "Real difficulties can be overcome; it is only the imaginary ones that are unconquerable" was the moment when I stopped taking my imagination for granted. Whenever going against a challenging goal, I'd always become pessimistic about overcoming the obstacles, so the more I gained confidence about past situations the better I felt. My ability to take heed on Jim Rohn's advice and make it more understanding was definitely a big motivation towards me. I figured if I stayed ambitious about improving and learning, I'll be in my prime was faster than I expect it. I felt better after learning from Thomas Jefferson that "He who knows nothing is closer to the truth than he whose mind is filled with falsehoods and errors", mainly because his information was like what my life revolved around. Back when I first became aware of how valuable life was, I've heard from many motivational speakers mention to "unlearn what you currently have in your mind and refill it with more meaningful information" which was my biggest fear only because of how long the process would take. Moments after pondering on their advice, I realized how much I didn't know so whenever I decided to better my life, acquiring new data in mind wasn't hard at all. I noticed how the more I seek to find valuable life changing information the more I received.

Write down what you've learned

1. _____

2. _____

3. _____

"IQKJ"

*"Goals are not only absolutely necessary to motivate us.
They are essential to really keep us alive"*
-Robert H. Schuller

I had such a great realization about my work ethic after being well informed about this advice only because, the times when I did to set goals they were my most productive moments, especially while enjoying the feeling of accomplishing something that I really thought was worthwhile. Since realizing that growth was necessary I haven't been the same since in terms of wasting time, which resulted from accepting the fact that I wanted to be as successful as my next breath. As crazy as it may seems, I often forget about the "only the strong survive" phrase which was rare only because I thought that it was possible to stay motivated from finding my gift, but little did I know that being courageous on unfortunate days was truly necessary. From the moment I started to deal with the world as it was, the less pressure I felt because by me being so far in my dreams and accomplishing many of my goals, the more I started to appreciate the reality of wisdom, despite of any situation. I knew that I had to live with this mind of mines until I perished so I figured why not value it and see how far it can take me by continually executing new ideas that I've acquired. My intentions to be great was all I could've dwell on at times and I knew that it was only because of my past experiences with working so hard, so I figured why not keep seeing what I was capable of in times of not being sure if my success was going to come. I've heard from many of people who I admired that "real success is all about your next move" so I began using that advice to help me keep hope.

Write down what you've learned

1. _____

2. _____

3. _____

"IQKJ"

*"Life has no meaning the moment you
lose the illusion of being eternal"*
-Jeal-Paul Sartre

I became massively thankful that I had ran across this information without having to learn the hard way or just being loss with someone having to force this ideology on me. Since learning that it was possible to harness my will power and let it help develop more of a meaningful life to me is when I started to positively take advantage of things that had a big impact on my life. I felt as if this one opportunity of mines would allow me to be as valuable as I pleased mainly because it was so rare in my generation to be an Author and to actually be good at it so my main motivation to continue doing so was my growth process. While contemplating on putting all I had into my craft was what allowed me to appreciate the reality of knowing that my destiny depended upon my decisions. The mentality of knowing that God didn't bring me so far just to leave me has had a big impact on the way I perceived temporary dissatisfactions which I believe I struggled to understand after noticing how good I thought I was doing when it came to my career. Since pouring my soul when it came to showing my audience what I was really capable of was all I needed at times because had If I been shy and wanted to keep all the valuable advice that I was receiving to myself, I wouldn't have never realized my genius potential. The Henry Rollins quote "you need a little bit of insanity to do great things" had made me more comfortable with my writing process because I always felt as if I worked hard enough on what I promised to myself I'll soon be in line for living the life that I'm destined to.

Write down what you've learned

1. _____

2. _____

3. _____

"IQKJ"

"Singleness of purpose is one of the chief essentials for success in life, no matter what may be ones aim."
- John D. Rockefeller

The appreciation for my ability to get this far as an Author, wasn't all that I became proud about after running across this information but the discipline and consistency that I persevered through while not being sure on what I wanted to do with my career. By me simply having goals to achieve while still focusing on my craft had become more of something to talk about because at times when I'd reminisce on the past, I remember days of not being sure if I wanted to live the next few minutes so now that I feel so purposeful, there's nothing I'd replace the appreciation with. From the moment I made it my obligation to make myself proud by accomplishing certain things, were my greatest understanding about knowing what I was willing to do if my mind was set on it, because as I've heard from many of my idols that success is based off how you feel on the inside and my natural ability to do the right thing wouldn't have let me ignored that advice. The reality of know that time heals everything was slowly becoming my main reason to stay resilient when it came to overcoming small obstacles, only because I knew how foolish I'll be if I gave up on my audience when my craft had built such a strong and firm relationship with them. The thought of continually being versatile when it came to my craft was exactly what I needed to master because I've had many of my audiences complimenting me on how good of a job I've done but I realized that the uniqueness about my craft was having many topics to touch on so I figured why not study the phrase "Repetition is the mother of learning" just to see how beneficial it is.

Write down what you've learned

1. _____

2. _____

3. _____

"IQKJ"

The ability to simplify means to eliminate
the unnecessary so that the necessary may speak"
-Hans Hofmann

As obvious as this advice had seemed, I never heard it worded this way, but later on it brought me many ideas on why my style of writing was so important and to be freely when it came to informing others on not just doing something but actually doing it the right way based on how you feel. The reality of finding peace of mind when life seemed challenging was by far my biggest accomplishment I've ever achieved because at times, I never thought that I'll be able to understand my situation by simply choosing one thought over another and by doing so I began using this method to stay balanced on all levels of my life. The idea just wouldn't resonate in my mind that God put us here to be average or ordinary, so I used that simple factor to motivate me whenever I felt as if I wasn't doing my best which was by far the greatest understanding I ran across. Since learning from Walt Whitman that "Simplicity is the glory of expression" I haven't been the same since in terms of worrying about over thinking when it came to not being sure if being great was possible. The understanding of me and others having different aspirations had allowed me to feel comfortable when it came to knowing that it was okay for me to want the more expensive things in life without feeling bad about it. My intentions to become more of a valuable individual was all I dwelled on in times of being alone and the pessimistic side will sometimes remind me of how challenging it'll be so I'd always reflect back on Soren Kier-loegard quote that's says "Anxiety is the dizziness of freedom" which reminded me that I was on the right track.

Write down what you've learned

1.
———————————————————————————————————————

2.
———————————————————————————————————————

3.
———————————————————————————————————————

"IQKJ"

*"The Art of being wise is the art
of knowing what to overlook"
-William James*

This philosophy had slowly made me realize how important it was to be clear about things that I gave my attention
to because I always felt as if I over analyzed every situation
I ran across, not knowing that I needed balance in
those circumstances. By me not ever wanting to disrespect my craft
in terms of not giving all I've had when it came to doing research on
an idea, was all I needed to be aware of while trying to stay wise. The
ideology of trying to evolve more as a human being was so motivating to me that I decided to start appreciating my existence more until
I actually grew with this craft of mines. The Pema Chardon quote
"Nothing ever goes away until it teaches us what we know" was exactly what I needed to stay aware of while wondering why I wasn't
progressing in situations where I knew I should've been further in,
which was also life changing later on because I thought that the uni-
verse had forgot about me, not knowing I needed to grow more. Becoming more of an asset to my audience was what I contemplated
on when not being sure if I wanted to challenge myself to growing,
which later on gave me a reality check about my future.
Harold J. Smith philosophy "More people would learn from their
mistakes if they weren't to busy denying them" was also something
I cherished when it came to understanding certain reasons on why
I haven't progressed in my career. Immediately after running across

Harold's advice I decided to focus more on what I had control over, rather than my mistakes on not taking my craft as seriously because from the moment I knew I couldn't go a day without getting inspiration from something is when I knew that writing was meant for me.

Write down what you've learned

1. _____

2. _____

3. _____

"IQKJ"

*"Wisdom is the power to put our time and
our knowledge to proper use"*
- Tom Watson

I felt so relieved after knowing that wisdom is part of knowing what you don't want, so the more confirmation I received about it, the better I approached my craft in ways to give by far best advice to my audience. Since being aware of John C. Maxwell philosophy which says "Creativity requires willingness to look stupid" is when I knew that as long as I took this advice and used it strategically, I couldn't fail. I felt as if I was blessed to be aware of the phrase "When life gives you lemons, make lemonade" at such a young age because I used it to take advantage of things that was in my possession in good ways, which helped me with boredom at times. By me keeping the "What's the worst that can happen" mentality has become a main reason for taking challenging risk when it came to sacrificing free time for the betterment of my career. I had the ideology of "either I proceed or I don't" and of course I wanted the better but the mentality seemed much more sustainable when it came to my process for creating. The reality of me already feeling ahead of the curve when it came to treating others how I wanted to be treated had made me feel better for all of the knowledge that I'm currently acquiring about motivation because I felt as if when it does settle in, I'll be way further than I ever imagined. Right before I stopped struggling with the mentality of taking myself too seriously Is when I found out that it was possible to be balanced with my creative pace and not let others slow me down by saying "I work too much".

Write down what you've learned

1. _____

2. _____

3. _____

"IQKJ"

"Knowledge is learning something everyday,
wisdom is letting go of something everyday"
- Zen Proverb

I was more confident than ever after acquiring this advice because I've recently heard Jack Ma mention on interview with (CNBC) that "Smart people know what to want, wise people know what they don't want". Since being very clear about what I didn't want, the better I felt about focusing specifically on one thing which was writing. The ability to be my worst critic had benefited me in so many ways when it came to staying away from things that I didn't want because the more I worked on my craft, the more time I had to continue getting better at what I did. While many people doubted me by basically saying "It's easy to get rich, the hardest part is staying rich" which I absolutely believed was true but I always had in my mind that the discipline that I used to become rich, could be there for me when my money wasn't so I appreciated their input but I just decided to stay away from them until I got to where I wanted to be. The reality of actually taking my craft one day at a time was also a major motivator for me to forget about being overwhelmed by others. It was a challenge to motivate myself everyday but I rarely let others opinions about me writing everyday get the best of me only because I knew it was going to pay off in the long run. The great question of "Are you living or just existing" was something to dwell on whenever I felt as if I wasn't progressing and it'll always help me to find new creative ways to stay focused on what I believed which was making myself very valuable to God as well as my audience. By me originally wanting to inspire others had left me with no room to complain when it came to putting the work in to be where I wanted.

Write down what you've learned

1. _____

2. _____

3. _____

"IQKJ"

*"In a crowded marketplace, fitting in is a failure.
In a busy marketplace, not standing out is
the same thing as being invisible"*
–Seth Godin

This specific information had instantly gave me a new perspective on studying myself as well as my craft. By me not cheating myself and staying honest whenever rereading what I've written had made my level of satisfaction rise, which was rare but I knew that it was meant to be only because I had worked so hard on doing what I believed was my purpose for being here. The thought of not being known as an Author was something that I couldn't dwell on for long periods of time because I stayed aware of knowing how rare my craft were and how much work I've put in while studying my abilities. I felt as if my wardrobe had played a huge role in my audience perception of me so the way I dressed was based off how I really felt about the brand because I've known that the creators of those items had worked so hard. Since raising my standards on knowing how beneficial I wanted my craft to be was by far the best decision that I could've made because by having others mention to me that I've helped change their perspective on life had always encouraged me to work hardest than I previously did which was half of what I was really capable of. Receiving confirmation in this day of age was all I needed to stay motivated because I realized that there's been too many people before me who had succeeded massively by acquiring certain information that I'm currently running across, so my main challenge was trying not to become naive when it came to learning which was something that I overcame by simply wanting to be more of a service from God.

Write down what you've learned

1. _____

2. _____

3. _____

"IQKJ"

"The most rewarding things you can do in life are often the ones that look like they cannot be done"
–Arnold Palmer

Hearing advice like this from someone like Arnold was exactly where my focus needed to be, only because it made me realize how doing the impossible while being around doubters was so necessary for them as well as myself. From the moment I felt deserving about going as far as my gift took me is when I took a different approach on the way I let others treat me, which means I stayed cool but I no longer let anyone tell me what I couldn't do. At times, the capabilities that I've seen for myself was so clear to the point where I knew how foolish I'd be if I got drowned by the overwhelming comments of what I couldn't do by others. My refusal to let success make a fool of me had motivated me so much in terms of appreciating all the times that I've spent on not just studying but also trying to learn the levels of success and not letting it go to waste. Early on, thankfully I learned from Jim Rohn to let go of my blame list which means life, others, or anything else that I let hold me back mentally. I suddenly started to use the power of choice which also helped me start making better decisions. The thought about what's the point of becoming successful if I can't enjoy it, had balanced me to the point where all I wanted to do was actually achieve my goals in peace.

Write down what you've learned

1. _____

2. _____

3. _____

"IQKJ"

*"To understand the heart and mind of a person,
look not at what he has already achieved,
but at what he aspires to be"
-Kahill Gibran*

I used this information to help my audience realize how powerful of a person I planned on being and what legacy that I wanted to leave behind. Back when I first started writing, I had no intentions on how impactful I was going to be to others so when I finally gained that awareness, I treated becoming valuable to others like it was all I had. The fact that I figured out what I wanted to do in life and started practicing it with a passion had blew my mind every time I thought about it only because I stayed discipline and committed to something for so long. I had already known that I wasn't going back to my old lifestyle so I figured why not focus so hard on becoming an influential individual. The thrill and excitement that I received when following how I felt on the inside just to put something on earth that wasn't here before had only allowed me to love and accept more of who I was made to be. Since learning that humans learn more from others differences way more than similarities had become another reason on why I embraced my creativity, just to show others how rare they can be. The simple understanding of knowing that I can't be beat at being me was all I needed to know while pondering on what was necessary to say while writing. My ability to make the best out of most of my situations had made me start appreciating my current circumstances way more until I got to where I wanted to be, so the process of being influential didn't seem that much overwhelming only because I knew what I was capable of.

Write down what you've learned

1. _____

2. _____

3. _____

"IQKJ"

"To live is to suffer, to survive is to find
one meaning in the suffering"
- Friedrich Nietzsche

This philosophy seemed to be exactly what I needed to help me cope with days when I felt as if I got too far ahead of myself, but which later on made me realize that I was on the right track by finding something that I enjoyed in this world of suffering. The idea of serving as an inspiration to others who aspired to emulate my craft had always reminded that I must become better every day if I want to leave such a great legacy when it came to writing. By me always having that urge to create and improve on paper was all of the reasoning that I needed just to maintain the idea of knowing that my craft won't get boring to me if I continued to find ways on how it could help the world. The "Better late than never" mentality is what kept me level headed in terms of knowing that I have already found my purpose, so by me continuing on this journey and doing the right thing was all I needed to worry about. I started to let Dalia Lama simple philosophy "Remember that sometimes not getting what you want is a wonderful stroke of luck" get the best of me and I later on realized, had I not became aware of this information, I would've became miserable because I thought that I deserved to get whatever I wanted since I worked for it, not knowing it could've been bad for me. Never in years would I have thought that my life could be remembered as an Author, so after realizing that it was possible, I had immediately made it my objective to appreciate the opportunity of doing what I loved for a living.

Write down what you've learned

1. _____

2. _____

3. _____

"IQKJ"

"Fanaticism consist of rebuilding your effort
when you have forgotten your aim"
-George Santayana

Thankfully I haven't loss my effort to accomplish things that I set out to achieve, like the goal of not giving up when the road got tough, which was something so challenging that I set my mind to. I did fantasize so much on reaping the benefits on all I had worked for, so I was okay in terms of knowing that my future was going to be bright if I continued to work. I've always had the "I have nothing to lose, but everything to gain" mentality while in the middle of my writing career so I rarely struggled with letting others know how serious I was about succeeding with my specific craft. It wasn't until I ran across Charles F. Ketterling advice that said "Believe and act as if it were impossible to fail" which really made me want to move way more strategically on days when I decided to challenge myself. I felt as if my craft would always stay relevant even when I perished because in the process of becoming an Author I'd always hear the saying "It's not about what you do for yourself but what you can do for others in times of need" and after noticing how great I could be with my legacy had only made me become more thankful for doing what I loved for a living which was letting others know how possible success was. When it came to my writing process, I had always stuck with the "If it ain't broke, don't fix it" mentality and as time passed on by, my creativity level had risen massively so I always had new content for my audience. My intentions were to always give my all to something that I really cared about, whether it was relationships, fashion, or sports they never gave me the same sense of fulfillment that writing did which let me know how dedicated I was to helping others.

Write down what you've learned

1. _____

2. _____

3. _____

"IQKJ"

"The most I'm important single ingredient in the formula of success is knowing how to get along with people."
–Teddy Roosevelt

The feeling of surpassing those previous doubts I've had about not being sure if others were going to accept my craft, was by far my greatest achievements ever mainly because I didn't want to feel a negative way about those who doubted what I loved doing for a living. I always strayed away from things that had a threat on my peace of mind, and that was mainly because I couldn't operate through my career by knowing that it was easy to get distracted so I just decided to focus on what I had control over. At certain moments in the process of my career I felt like the act of continuing to tell others around me that "becoming successful is like a marathon" was always a waste of time especially after I'll reminisce on the saying "most people won't see nor believe it until it actually happens". Since hearing T.I. mention in a Tidal-Vision Co-cavison interview that"It's hard to put a lot of effort into something and make it look effortless but it's not hard to make something look effortless that you ain't gotta put no effort in" my attitude towards my craft hasn't been the same since and it was a blessing because had I not ran across that valuable information I don't think I could've maintained my work ethic by having a bunch of too supportive people around. The thought of my true success not having a date on it had humbled me in times of being impatient which eventually allowed me to appreciate my existence way more than ever because when I look back on certain situations I tried to rush it didn't work out that well for me.

Write down what you've learned

1. _____

2. _____

3. _____

"IQKJ"

"Patience is necessary, and one cannot
reap immediately where one has sown."
- Soren Kierkegaard

Right after reading this quote, the thought of being persistent was the only thing that had crossed my mind which I believed was a good thing because I knew if I started to become more patient, I'll have to dedicate my time to something else just to stay satisfied with knowing that my time wasn't being wasted. At times when I struggled with thinking that God had forgot about me had become most of my miserable moments because I felt like there was no hope for me but the idea of knowing that patience was necessary when it came to my career had made me feel less overwhelmed until gaining a better sense of myself and what I was actually capable of. I had to cope with the "Delay isn't denial" mentality and it'll always get the best of me when I felt as if I was out of options or my craft wasn't going the pace that I expected but little did I know, all I had to do was keep going which always allowed me to enjoy the process more. There was certain information that I ran across where I knew without even writing it down, I'll be able to remember it forever like when I'll contemplate on Jim Rohn mentioning in a seminar that "Success is something you attract by the person you become" which was something that stayed on my mind whenever I felt like being lazy and my time was running out.

Write down what you've learned

1. _____

2. _____

3. _____

"IQKJ"

"With realization of one's own potential
and self- confidence in one's ability,
one can build a better world."
-Dalai Lama

This advice had become great information to run to whenever I needed a reality check. I figured that even if others weren't affected by my craft the goal was to help them look at the world differently, so my mentality would still be healthy only because once before I used writing for therapeutic reasons and it turned into a career for me. Since becoming so true to my purpose, and almost everything I've encountered with, my writing ability was on my mind so I stayed observant to what I felt that was beneficial to my craft. I had a great level of realism about what I was good at so when it came to having impact on others, I focused so hard on believing it was possible way before trying to put it in writing form. I knew if I ever stopped writing before I reached where I wanted to be, my career would've been in a world of trouble mainly because without constantly motivating myself about possibilities, I wouldn't be nowhere close to where I am today. The feeling of being a natural born leader had kept me focused on doing all I had in my power and that was to keep taking heed on valuable information like the simple understanding of knowing that there's always a way to overcome what you are going through if you get more information on it. From the moment I became aware of knowing that my attitude towards played a huge role in what I wanted to become, I stopped taking most of my chill time for granted and began using it to focus more on becoming the change I wanted to see in the world rather than just being satisfied with what I presented. The more I started to surround myself with valuable information the better my understanding skills became whenever coping with the thought of being average.

Write down what you've learned

1. _____

2. _____

3. _____

"IQKJ"

"Ability may get you to the top, but it takes
character to keep you there."
– John Wooden

The way I processed this information wasn't the same as my previous times so I knew I couldn't go no wrong with my understanding about it. Thankfully, I was taught at an early age to treat others how I want to be treated so I knew whenever I made it to the top I know I'll still have to maintain the thought of that Golden Rule or not I'll definitely be playing myself. Since I came to the clear understanding of knowing that I wanted to change the world and have fun doing it, had helped me know more on what I was actually spending my time on. Whenever pondering on valuable information, I always looked back on when I came to the understanding of how we all have 24 hours a day, and it's all about how we use them, I noticed how it'll instantly put me back in grind mode. I stayed with the mentality of knowing that life wasn't supposed to be easy so why not continue challenging myself to do what I wanted even if I wasn't conscious of my hard work eventually paying off. I knew my work ethic wouldn't be the same since reading from TD Jakes book called (Instinct) that "If you don't define yourself, your enemies will define you" which massively changed my life only because I've never heard it worded that way and most importantly it gave me a new way to start strategizing my work ethic. I noticed how most of my growth came when I started figuring out what I didn't want to be and the fear of not becoming those things had motivated me to get as far away as possible from that mentality, which eventually helped me start noticing what I did want to focus on.

Write down what you've learned

1. _____

2. _____

3. _____

"IQKJ"

*"Real generosity toward the future lies in
giving all to the present"*
–Albert Camus

I knew that my priorities were definitely in place after receiving this advice, mainly because it gave me confirmation on knowing that it's literally okay to give my craft all I had as long as I did it in a strategic way. I became less skeptical about giving all of my creativity away when I ran across Maya Angelou philosophy which said "You can't use up creativity. The more you use, the more you have" and it seemed to be very true because my books were examples. The continuous of excitement of knowing that my craft was going to pay off seemed to be a reason I worked so tireless at times. I constantly contemplated on knowing that the more I worked, the more discipline I'll be and the more appreciation others will have for me for inspiring them. In the past, I've experienced a large amount of neglect so when I got very comfortable with writing and started to gain an audience, I began cherishing my support system only because I knew that my craft benefited had us both. Just the thought of remaining in my current circumstances after putting so much work in writing didn't seem as satisfying to me so I knew I had to do all I was capable of just to make sure my craft was good enough to spread to the world. By me never losing the motivation of writing like I had something to prove, has left me with shocking reactions while doing the edit process because I knew how great of something I was becoming by dedicating my time to it. At times I felt as if nothing was more important than succeeding as an Author because I still had to live with myself, so by not working towards or achieving my goal wasn't something I wanted to regret so I made the "care for myself first before others" mentality work in a beneficial way. By me not tolerating any wasted time from myself had opened my eyes on how serious I was about my career and what I planned on leaving behind which was something I wanted to realize since becoming an Author.

Write down what you've learned

1. _____

2. _____

3. _____

"IQKJ"

"First step towards getting somewhere is to decide that you are not going to stay where you are."
-JP Morgan

My understanding to appreciate my work ethic had definitely settled in after running across this advice only because I previously made the decisions to focus a large amount of time on writing, just to see a new outcome. Many sacrifices I've made had also helped me to stay aware of knowing that there was no turning around from what I envisioned while being a committed Author. Basically I put myself in a "all or nothing" situation but I later on realized that I can only fail if I decided to give up on what I believed. Certain methods had seemed unbelievable until I actually put them into action like filling my mind up with valuable ideas and information just so I wouldn't suffer with being overwhelmed by minor problems. My vision became so clear the more I sacrificed my time for writing which I believed came from staying conscious of the Bible phrase "Walk by faith, not by sight". My instincts made me stay obsessed with constantly working on my craft so the more improvement I've seen the more grateful I felt to continue doing what I loved. Since noticing the difference between being patient and actually wasting my time had later on made me value my time more. By me starting to live each day as if it was my last had also helped me to really give all I had to my work ethic while creating. The simple phrase "Be the change you want to see in the world" gave me more reasons to not slow down with what

I was creating so I finally came to the understanding of how my craft was going to get me where I needed to go.

Write down what you've learned

1. _____

2. _____

3. _____

"IQKJ"

"No man knows how bad he is till he
has tried very hard to be good."
- C.S Lewis

I mmediately began using this advice to help me appreciate what I presented to my audience in my prior books. I never felt as if my craft was bad, I just stayed honest with myself and noticed it could've been better. The reality of turning nothing into something had always motivated me to become creative as I wanted to be. By me not dwelling on excuses, I became more willing to work as smart as I could've just to make what I presented more valuable to others. While writing with a purpose, I knew deep down I couldn't fail only because I felt as if so many people related to my thoughts, they've just never seen it on paper before. At times when I reflected on how much work I've put it, it'll instantly put me in a better mood which was only a sign of me finally having something to be appreciative about. When I finally decided to make part of my craft based on letting my audience know how life wasn't so overwhelming once finding your purpose, is when I became more thankful about becoming more known as an Author. The thought of dying while trying to make my dreams come true had made me feel better than just sitting at home feeling sorry for the God approving moves that I didn't have enough of courage to make which was some advice that I've recently became aware of. I've heard too many massively successful people say "Stay in your own lane and work hard at doing what you love" which was the meaning behind their great fortunes, so I knew I'd be a fool had I not taken their advice seriously. The blessing to wake up every morning gave me all the hope I needed, simply because it's like I was always given a second chance get better at what I loved.

Write down what you've learned

1. _____

2. _____

3. _____

"IQKJ"

*"Don't forget – no one else sees the world
the way you do, so no one else can tell the
stories that you have to tell."*
– Charles de Lint

I had such a better feeling to continue creating after hearing this advice from another successful writer. In the process of writing my last two books, I never dwelled on how powerful my perspective was to the world, which was only because I became too excited that I actually created something while not knowing my true value. I stayed aware of knowing that the success I wanted wasn't going to come overnight but I balanced my impatient feelings by knowing that all the work I've put in with writing was eventually going to pay off. Since hearing from Jim Rohn that "If you struggle to make something clear for someone else it helps to make it more clear for you" and from that point on, I knew that I was definitely on the right track to becoming something very valuable only because I had dedicated so much of my time while trying to make my craft more relatable to others. By me sticking with writing through the good and the bad, had became a big result of my discipline so I always felt as if I was to ever stop writing it'll be because I was no longer interested in inspiring others with what I learned, which was something that stole my joy every time I thought about it. My ability to control what I was able to had also helped better my mood when feelings overwhelmed me, like having the sense to pick up a book when things immediately irritated me. I'll go in creative mode once again, then simply use that anger and make it more logical in writing form. It wasn't too many people that I was aware of that had used the same creative process as me so I stuck with it and later on realized how spending time on studying how I overcame challenges to present to my audience was also beneficial to me.

Write down what you've learned

1. _____

2. _____

3. _____

"IQKJ"

"We cannot always build the future for our youth, but we can build our youth for the future" -Franklin D. Roosevelt

This advice had helped me develop an even stronger sense to stay connected to the youth, especially to the ones who admired my craft. I stayed honest with myself by knowing that everyone wasn't interested in what I had created so by just sticking to what I knew, was more inspiring and helped me feel better. Since hearing Jim Rohn mention in a seminar that "If you start young, the future is already promised to you" I haven't had the same perspective towards the youth as well as myself so I figured if I studied it, and let my audience know how beneficial it can be, they'll be way more discipline in the long run. Whenever I reflected on my past, I became so thankful that my life went the way that it did, despite of the ups and downs only because I can now appreciate where my commitment to writing has gotten me. By me not having any regrets, I look at certain goals that I wanted to achieve back then and realize that they were attainable if I had the guidance of doing so, which now makes me understand the power of seeking knowledge. Now that I'm an Author, I take courage in trying to show others how to avoid certain mistakes I've made and as cliché as it may sound, it makes all the sense to me because I feel as if when others become aware of making a better decision they have a bigger possibility of doing just that. My ability to know exactly what I wanted and put it in goal form had always helped me cope with days when I felt as if my craft had lost value. Another objective for my craft was to let my audience and the youth read what I've created and find hints of what they were unaware of only to know more of what they were capable of.

Write down what you've learned

1. _____

2. _____

3. _____

"IQKJ"

"The true measure of a man is how he treats someone who can do him absolutely no good" –Samuel Johnson

My initial thought after receiving this advice was "Why didn't I build my confidence around this information early on" only because I felt like the act of treating others right was just part of me. I learned from Michael Jordan how to focus more on my abilities after reading his quote which said "I've always believed that if you put the work in the results will come" and I later on started to pick up the wisdom for why knowing myself is so important. The reality of wanting to make peace my priority after working so hard on my craft had gave me more drive than ever because I knew that my concentration level needed to be balanced while moving through my days. The "You never too old to learn and never too young to teach" mentality was where my career stayed elevated only because I always felt as if my writing style were for those who understood some basics for success. The thought of continually letting my gift make way more for me was by far the best thing that I could've showed those who doubted my reason for being here. Thankfully, I let go of trying to force myself to learn everything others suggested for me and just stuck to my idealistic way of acquiring knowledge. Since deciding what's more valuable to know has lessened the pressure on me and has allowed me to have multiple options when knowing who to receive advice from. I kept forgetting the phrase "It's not where you've been but, all about where your going" and suddenly I started to let the rhythm of knowing myself fade away, then I'd regain control by acknowledging it.

Write down what you've learned

1. _____

2. _____

3. _____

"IQKJ"

"By being yourself, you put something
wonderful in the world that was not there before"
–Edwin Elliot

s common as this advice had seemed, I used it to help me refresh my memory on how important being influential was. The thought of being a consistent writer and knowing that one day I'll have an impact on so many people had inspired me because I've heard many successful mention how they had no idea that their craft was going to affect so many people. Whenever sitting alone, I had often questioned myself like "If others have made it to become massively by staying committed, why can't I?" and that question seemed to motivate me to ignore all of what others thought negatively about my craft. I stayed conscious of knowing that anything I wanted to achieve, I had to literally deserve it, so by working hard on my craft was definitely going to solidify my proof to help me receive the fortunes I wanted. Since having the courage that this career of mines was really going to work, had made me start approaching life in different ways because this was the only time in my life where I felt as if I was doing something productive so I continued giving writing all I had and later on it became effortless to me. The idea of trying to help change the way others think had seemed much more important than changing the way I wrote every time someone pointed out a flaw in my writing ability.

Write down what you've learned

1. _____

2. _____

3. _____

"IQKJ"

*"You are here to enrich the world
and you impoverish if you forget that errand"
-Woodrow Wilson*

The inspiration I've had while absorbing this advice was undeniably my favorite piece of information I ever received, mainly because it allowed me to realize that as long as I have this passion for writing, I'll stay wealthy and as relevant as I want to be, especially if my audience appreciate my craft more than ever before. By me continuing to repeat what had worked was also by far the best thing I could've done only because if I focused on instantly trying to find new ways to do things, I would've easily loss all of the motivation I've had for being consistent with this writing ability of mines. Things that I gave my heart to like writing didn't seem that complicated to me mainly because I always felt like I'll eventually understand it by constantly working on it and as time passed I became clear about what I set out to do. I eventually found my peace of mind in the pursuit of going after my dreams so I knew that if I was to ever stop creating my craft, part of the world would lose hope. By me writing as if my audience were already part of me had made most them who stayed updated on my content feel like they knew how valuable I was going to be by doing such a great job. I knew that many people around me would think I'm crazy just for believing in myself so massively but I stayed level headed by continuing to contemplate on the phrase "Everybody likes something, you just have to keep working hard and see". After pondering on that information for such a long time I started to slowly fade away from my crowd of doubters just to focus on how good my craft could be by actually overcoming what others thought was impossible.

Write down what you've learned

1. _____

2. _____

3. _____

"IQKJ"

"Only through art can we emerge from
ourselves and know what another person sees."
- Marcel Proust

My perspective towards my career was insanely different after running across this information and I believe that it was only because it made me realize how you really have to be active in this world just to get your art noticed. Being dedicated to something as inspiring as writing had kept me relevant on days when I thought I was forgot about, which I believed is what kept me going because by knowing that I changed most of my audience perspectives on life was all the motivation I needed for the time being. The Darrin Patrick quote "Discipline is rarely enjoyable but almost always profitable" had molded me into a nonstop focusing mode when it came to my craft because by coming so far, I've seen how much better writing made me feel emotional wise. There hasn't been a feeling in this world yet that I cherished more than finding my purpose for being here, which now makes me want to spread this advice to the world on how I'm so motivated to keep going. I couldn't think of anything but progressing when it came to writing and I believed that it was only because I sacrificed so much time away from doing things that I once thought was fun, just to feel satisfied about being active. Thankfully, I wasn't a fool and just believed that being active didn't always mean that my skills for writing was developing, I just stayed with a healthy mindset of knowing that I have to change in order to see change. I wanted to feel grateful about the achievements that I really worked for, so in certain situations I made it my obligation to give all I had to writing and every time while doing so I seen it pay off.

Write down what you've learned

1. _____

2. _____

3. _____

"IQKJ"

"The reading of all good books is like a conversation
with the finest minds of past centuries."
- Rene Descartes

This information forced me to realize how there's two ways that I can benefit from it which was, use it to help better my writing by having rare conversations with people from the past and to help my audience understand how valuable it would be to them if they decided to take heed and maybe go further than me. The reality of knowing that I was really contributing something to society had always motivated me to where I needed to be, especially when it came to focusing on the optimistic side of things. I had a great passion for studying valuable advice and eventually reaping the benefits by realizing that I was actually becoming smarter by knowing that I maintained this ability of mines, I'll have a huge impact on others how books currently have on me. Since coming to the sense of "Everything happens for a reason" I started to maneuver through life in different ways, which later on payed off for me by noticing that the more I read, the less situations I'll have to worry about. The appreciation for my growth was all I needed to know at times at times, which made my commitment for reading much more soothing and more eager to attract success by becoming a better person. I always felt as if I had great conversations with those who were interested in talking to me and I felt this way long before becoming an Author so now my conversations with myself is documented and also now able to satisfy those who enjoy my time. By me being so anxious for growth had become a main reason for why I never loss the great thought of treating others I wanted to be treated, which always dwelled on my mind whenever I thought the process for my success wasn't coming faster than I've thought.

Write down what you've learned

1. _____

2. _____

3. _____

"IQKJ"

"The future of publishing is about having connections to readers and the knowledge of what those readers want" -Seth Godin

My way of approaching my audience was definitely settled after running across this information because it allowed me to stop being a bit skeptical when it came to focusing so hard on will others accept the way I worded my craft. The actual day of telling my audience that hard work really pays off was a constant vision that I wanted to come true, because for a while when working so hard on my craft I sometimes felt as if it was ahead of its time but little did I know, whether others understood it or not, my craft will still be valuable for anyone if they just decided to take interest in it and my personality seemed to handle that part. I knew I had to balance the thought of others always critiquing my craft rather than congratulating me, but I only pondered on that thought when I put pressure on myself which was mainly because I never thought that anyone would take what I did so seriously so when I became aware that the world wasn't what I thought it was, it had really helped me to become more comfortable when creating. While fighting for my spot to make others understand me, had added a thrill of excitement when it came to challenging myself, which I believed was always my advantage because I believed in my work ethic as well as my talent so in my mind I knew I could've only failed myself. I stayed conscious of Benjamin Franklin philosophy which said "Diligence is the mother of luck" so I knew the more I worked on my craft, the luckier I'll be when it came to receiving opportunities from my audience only because writing seemed to be the only thing that satisfied my mentality at times.

Write down what you've learned

1. _____

2. _____

3. _____

"IQKJ"

"The greatest mistake we make is living in constant fear that we will make one."
– John C. Maxwell

This information had made me immediately realize why staying in creative mode was definitely an advantage for myself mainly because leaving it was the only time I felt fear about things that could've happened. Early on in my career, I did develop the skills that helped me understand fear, so I wasn't a fan of stressing over things that were completely out of my hands. I had always felt better by going through life simply creating books that I hoped to inspire others and slowly but surely it began to come true for me. The ability to take my plan so seriously had always given me a new meaning after feeling drained, so I couldn't too much worry about letting certain things get the best of me. The understanding that I received from working on my craft had become unexplainably inspiring at times, so I began using those experience just to live in the moment and later benefit so much from it. Since staying conscious of the phrase "The more you do, the more you get" had helped me noticed that even if I wasn't reaping the benefits from my craft, I was still building on my discipline which I believed was most important. The great fact of knowing that we live in a world that's full of possibilities as well as opportunities had me become more motivated with accepting the awareness of knowing that it's literally okay to keep putting more books out whenever being creative. All of the anxiety that I've previously had before becoming an Author, didn't affect me as much anymore so the better I began feeling about what I presented to the world, the more conformation it had gave me to really continue staying surrounded by what I had control over.

Write down what you've learned

1. _____

2. _____

3. _____

"IQKJ"

"The greatest use of life is to spend it for something that will outlast it" -William James

This advice had seemed so interesting and beneficial to the point that I knew by balancing my career and real life wasn't going to so overwhelming while trying to be in the need of others. The ability to share my inspiring thoughts with my wide range of audience had instilled in me that contributing something to the world can really be exciting if it's approached in the right way. Since staying aware of the phrase "By helping others were helping ourselves" my attitude towards humanity hasn't been the same which I believed was the main reasoning for me being here for such a long period of time. The reality of knowing that my craft was still going to be here even when I perished from this earth had literally motivated me to go as far as I could've with writing. I had a great feeling whenever I finished writing a book, that the only way I knew it was possible to maintain that ideology was to keep finding things to be inspired by and that simply came from knowing that I had others attention in such positive ways. The idea of working so hard that others couldn't ignore me, didn't seem that bad after knowing the real process of my craft. Thankfully, I didn't have the "I need to make mistakes in order to learn" mentality, I just stuck with what I knew and later on realized by writing every night I only became satisfied by knowing that I went as far as I thought about myself. My only challenge was to maintain the idea of becoming the best version of myself which was easily attainable only if I stayed aware of knowing that God wouldn't give me more than I could hold.

Write down what you've learned

1. _____

2. _____

3. _____

www.ingramcontent.com/pod-product-compliance
Lightning Source LLC
Chambersburg PA
CBHW070128230526
45472CB00004B/1473